student WORKBOOK

A2 Economics Multiple Choice

Cost and revenue	3
Market structures	10
Labour economics	23
Development economics	30
Macroeconomic policy	36
The global economy	46

Introduction

This collection of multiple-choice questions is designed to provide you as A2 Economics students with a valuable study companion to help improve your knowledge and understanding. The subject content is divided into sections and as far as possible mirrors the topics taught at A2 by the various examination boards. Not all the examination boards use multiple-choice questions in their scheme of assessment, but these questions will help to ensure that you thoroughly understand the concepts whichever specification you are following. As with the real examinations, it has been assumed that you have a sound knowledge of AS Economics concepts.

The material tested in the core areas is much the same across the examination boards. However, with some boards offering special option papers and some including topics or diagrams that others exclude, be careful to check the A2 specification for the examination board you are using before attempting the questions. The special option areas covered in this book are Labour Markets and Development Economics.

Each question has five options A–E, and you are expected to explain/justify/support your answer in the space given. In some cases this will involve a calculation or drawing a simple diagram. In some instances the diagram that has been given in the question could be adapted. When there is no need for an explanation or the chosen option takes the answer as far as possible, another related question has been asked as a follow-up.

Remember to read the questions carefully and look closely at the diagrams or the data that you have been given. If there are questions involving calculations, always check the answer with your

A2 Economics: Multiple Choice

calculator. You should not spend more than 3 minutes on each question and remember that in an examination a marker would award 1 mark for the correct answer and up to 3 more marks for the explanation. It is possible to pick up some marks in the explanation even if the answer you have chosen is wrong. Correct definitions and equations may be worth something, as they display knowledge of the topic being tested.

Once you have completed a section, either hand it your teacher to be marked or check it yourself against the answers given in the Teacher Notes. Here is a sample question and explanation for you to use as a guide.

Sample question

As the output increases for a firm in a perfectly competitive industry, its marginal revenue will:

A fall continuously
B fall at first, then rise
✓ C stay constant
D rise at first, then fall
E rise continuously

Explanation

In a perfectly competitive market, the price charged by each firm is constant at every level of output, as the demand curve is perfectly elastic. The marginal revenue is the addition to total revenue as a result of selling 1 extra unit of output. If the price is constant as output increases, the marginal revenue must equal the price and also be constant.

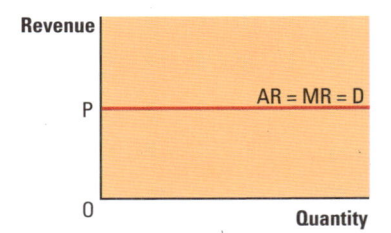

Acknowledgements

The author would like to thank the Welsh Joint Education Committee (WJEC) for allowing questions used in its previous A-level and AS multiple-choice examinations to be reproduced in this workbook. The responsibility for the answers rests entirely with the author.

The author would also like to thank Simon Harrison, Kiran Chopra and Martin Green who helped in checking the accuracy of both the questions and the answers. The author accepts responsibility for any errors or omissions that may be found in the book.

Cost and revenue

1 In the diagram, at which level of output will marginal revenue equal 0?

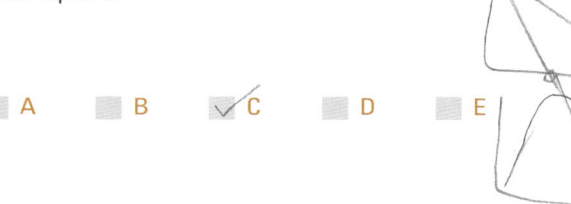

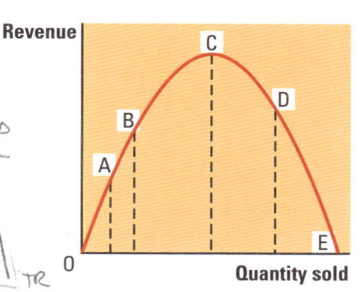

- A
- B
- ✓ C
- D
- E

Explanation: where MR = 0, price elasticity on demand curve = 1. at this point p × Q give maximum revenue/expenditure. At any higher level of output revenue is falling because MR is negative.

2 The table shows the demand schedule for a good.

It can be deduced from the schedule that marginal revenue is –£4 when price falls from:

- A £6 to £5
- B £5 to £4
- C £4 to £3
- ✓ D £3 to £2
- E £2 to £1

Price (£)	Quantity	R	MR
8	1	£8	£8
7	2	£14	£6
6	3	£18	£4
5	4	£20	£2
4	5	£20	£0
3	6	£18	£-2
2	7	£14	£-4
1	8	£8	£-6

Explanation: when p falls from £3 – £2, Revenue falls from £18 – £14 £. ∴ marginal revenue is £-4.

3 The diagram depicts the demand curve for a commodity and the marginal revenue associated with it. What is the price elasticity of demand at the price P?

- A zero
- B greater than zero but less than 1
- ✓ C 1
- D greater than 1 but less than infinity
- E infinity

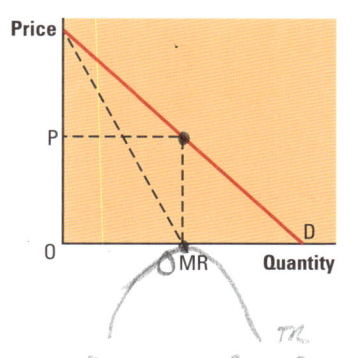

Explanation: at P → MR = 0 & total revenue is maximised. At this point on demand curve, ped = 1 as it is the curves mid point.

A2 Economics: Multiple Choice

4 If marginal revenue is always equal to average revenue, then:
- A the demand curve must be downward sloping
- ✓ B demand is perfectly elastic
- C demand is perfectly inelastic
- D the firm must be maximising its sales revenue
- E output is constant

Explanation: If MR=AR → there is infinite demand @ a given price. This means demand for product is perfectly elastic with a horizontal demand schedule (probably perfect competition).

5 If, when price is falling, marginal revenue starts to become negative, demand must have become:
- A unit elastic
- B relatively elastic
- ✓ C relatively inelastic
- D perfectly elastic
- E perfectly inelastic

Explanation: If a fall in price leads to a rise in quantity sold but a fall in revenue, this must mean that demand has become price inelastic (MR → negative). If price falls when demand is inelastic, MR also does, revenue as MR is -ve.

6 In the theory of the firm, the short run is distinguished from the long run by the assumption that in the short run:
- A all costs are variable
- B all factor inputs are variable
- C all factor inputs are fixed
- ✓ D at least one factor input is fixed
- E the firm must cover all of its costs

Explanation: In the short run, only one factor of production is variable - usually labor - the others, CL, are fixed. In long run all factors of production are variable.

Questions 7–11 refer to this diagram.

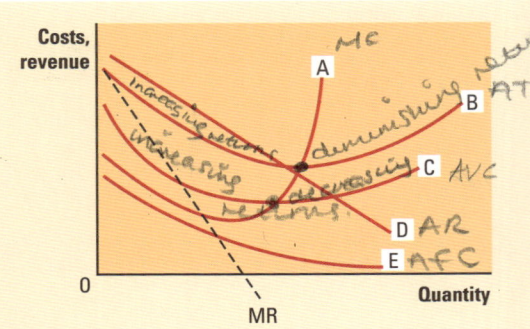

Costs, revenue
- A MC
- B ATC
- C AVC
- D AR
- E AFC

Increasing returns, diminishing returns, decreasing returns

MR, Quantity

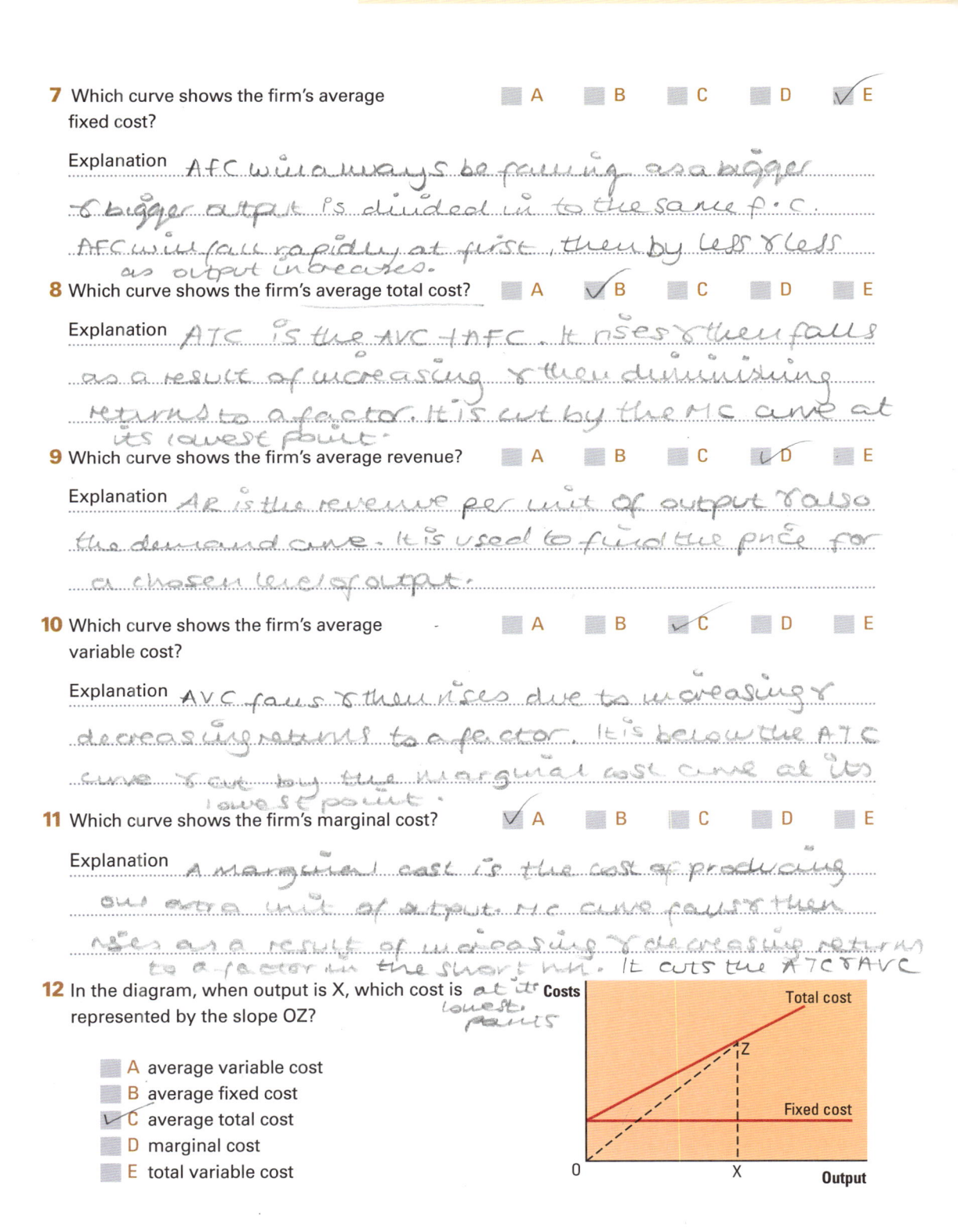

Cost and revenue

7 Which curve shows the firm's average fixed cost? □ A □ B □ C □ D ✓ E

Explanation AFC will always be falling as a bigger & bigger output is divided in to the same F.C. AFC will fall rapidly at first, then by less & less as output increases.

8 Which curve shows the firm's average total cost? □ A ✓ B □ C □ D □ E

Explanation ATC is the AVC + AFC. It rises & then falls as a result of increasing & then diminishing returns to a factor. It is cut by the MC curve at its lowest point.

9 Which curve shows the firm's average revenue? □ A □ B □ C ✓ D □ E

Explanation AR is the revenue per unit of output & also the demand curve. It is used to find the price for a chosen level of output.

10 Which curve shows the firm's average variable cost? □ A □ B ✓ C □ D □ E

Explanation AVC falls & then rises due to increasing & decreasing returns to a factor. It is below the ATC curve & cut by the marginal cost curve at its lowest point.

11 Which curve shows the firm's marginal cost? ✓ A □ B □ C □ D □ E

Explanation A marginal cost is the cost of producing one extra unit of output. MC curve falls & then rises as a result of increasing & decreasing returns to a factor in the short run. It cuts the ATC & AVC

12 In the diagram, when output is X, which cost is represented by the slope OZ? at its lowest points

□ A average variable cost
□ B average fixed cost
✓ C average total cost
□ D marginal cost
□ E total variable cost

A2 Economics: Multiple Choice

Explanation $\frac{TC}{Q} = AC$

The slope OZ can be measured by dividing ZX by OX. As ZX's = TC & OX is = Output, then $\frac{ZX}{OX} = AC$

13 A firm producing fountain pens has constant variable costs of £1.50 per unit and fixed costs of £100. If it produces 500 pens, what are its average costs?

- A 50p
- B £1.50
- ✓ C £1.70
- D £2.00
- E £2.50

$£1.50 \times 500 = 750 + 100 = 850$

$\frac{850}{500} = 1.7$ → £1.70

Explanation $AC = \frac{TC}{Q}$ or $AVC + AFC = £1.50 + \frac{100}{500} = 20p$

$£1.50 + 20p = £1.70$

14 Marginal cost is the:
- A lowest cost of producing a product
- B cost of production of the most inefficient firm in an industry
- C cost of production of the most efficient firm in an industry
- ✓ D change in total cost from producing one more unit
- E cost of production at which minimum profit is obtained by a firm

Why do marginal costs rise in the short run?

MC eventually rises in the SR because of diminishing returns to the variable factors of production - usually labour.

Questions 15–17 refer to this table, which shows the costs of a firm at various levels of output.

Production	Total cost (£)
0	100
1	110
2	120
3	130
4	140
5	150

15 The total fixed costs of the above firm are:
- A £0
- B £50
- C £75
- ✓ D £100
- E £150

Explanation identified at looking at output when it is 0 & these are £100.

Cost and revenue

16 What is the average variable cost of producing 3 units?

$\frac{30}{3} = 10$

- A £5
- ✓ B £10
- C £15
- D £20
- E £25

Explanation: Total cost of producing 3 units is £130. If F.C = £100, then V.C are £30. Average V.C is therefore £10 when divided by 3 units.

17 What is the average fixed cost of producing 4 units?

- A £15
- B £20
- ✓ C £25
- D £30
- E £100

Explanation: When output is 0, total cost = £100 = F.C. If 4 units are produced, the AFC are £100/4 = £25

18 The table shows the average cost of running a 1,300cc car over increasing annual mileages.

The change in average cost is mainly due to a fall in:

- A average variable cost
- B marginal cost
- C total cost
- ✓ D average fixed cost
- E fixed cost

Annual mileage	Average cost per mile
5,000	60p
10,000	40p
15,000	30p
20,000	25p
30,000	20p

Explanation: As mileage increases, the burden of F.C is spread over a greater no. of miles so the AFC fall. Road tax, insurance & depreciation are a small burden per mile & mileage increases.

19 A rise in average variable cost for a firm in the short run is caused by:

- A internal diseconomies of scale
- B decreasing returns to scale
- C a rise in average total cost
- ✓ D diminishing returns to a factor of production
- E external diseconomies of scale

A2 Economics: Multiple Choice

Explanation: Economies of scale & returns to scale are long run concepts when all f.o.p are variable. Rising SRAVC are caused by diminishing returns to a variable factor of production.

20 Normal profit is:
- A the total revenue minus total costs of a firm ✗ false
- ✓ B the minimum profit that the firm needs to stay in long-term production
- C average revenue multiplied by the quantity sold
- D the average level of profit earned by firms in the industry
- E the amount by which price exceeds the average cost of production

Explanation: Normal profit is the opp cost of resources. I.e. eco — if a firm is making just normal profits, then it is making just enough to stay in business in the LR.

21 In the long run, falling average costs that arise from within a firm are collectively referred to as:
- A increasing returns to a factor of production
- B constant returns to scale
- C external economies of scale
- D diminishing returns to a factor of production
- ✓ E internal economies of scale

Explanation: In the long run, all fop are variable. Reductions in long run average costs which arise from within a firm are called internal economies of scale.

22 The short-run marginal cost curve:
- A rises at first, then falls continuously as output rises
- B cuts the average fixed cost curve when it starts to rise
- C is always falling
- D cuts the average revenue curve at its lowest point
- ✓ E cuts the average variable cost curve at its lowest point

At what point does the marginal cost curve cut the average cost curve? SRMC curve also cuts the average cost curve at its lowest point.

Cost and revenue

23 A firm will shut down in the short run if the:

- A last unit sold adds the same amount to total revenue as it does to total costs
- B price is greater than the addition to costs as a result of producing 1 more unit P > MC
- ✓ C price is below the average variable cost P < AVC
- D price is less than the addition to costs as a result of producing 1 more unit P < MC
- E price is above the average variable cost but below the average total cost

Explanation: Where price is below AVC — it is not worth the firm producing in the SR. It is failing to cover v.c let alone fixed costs.

24 A firm is maximising profit when the:

- ✓ A last unit sold adds the same amount to total revenue as it does to total costs
- B price is greater than the addition to costs as a result of producing 1 more unit
- C price is equal to average variable cost
- D price is less than the addition to costs as a result of producing 1 more unit
- E price is above the average variable cost but below the average total cost

Explanation: A firm will profit maximise where MR = MC

25 A firm will produce in the short run but not in the long run when the:

- A last unit sold adds the same amount to total revenue as it does to total costs
- B price is greater than the addition to costs as a result of producing 1 more unit P > MC
- C price is equal to average variable cost P = VC
- D price is less than the addition to costs as a result of producing 1 more unit P < MC
- ✓ E price is above the average variable cost but below the average total cost

Explanation: A firm could survive in the SR by covering its variable costs, but in the long run it also has to cover both its FC & VC ie average total cost.

Market structures

1 When firms create barriers to entry for new firms, this is an aspect of:

- A market structure
- ✓ B market conduct
- C market performance
- D market concentration
- E market segmentation

Explanation: Creating a barrier to entry such as limit pricing is an act of market conduct because it is a policy designed to strengthen a firm's market position.

2 The extent to which firms minimise costs and attempt to be efficient and profitable is an aspect of:

- A market structure
- B market conduct
- ✓ C market performance
- D market power
- E market concentration

Explanation: When firms have achieved minimum costs or profit maximisation – example of market performance → something that has been achieved in the market.

3 The number of firms in an industry and their relative market shares is an aspect of:

- ✓ A market structure
- B market conduct
- C market performance
- D market failure
- E market segmentation

Explanation: A structure of an industry is often measured by the use of a concentration ratio: the percentage of the market controlled by eg the 5 largest firms.

4 Allocative efficiency requires price to equal:

- A average variable cost
- B average fixed cost
- C average total cost
- ✓ D marginal cost
- E marginal revenue

$AE = P = MC$

Explanation: The price that consumers are prepared to pay for a product (their valuation of it) is equal to the resource cost of producing it (MC).

Market structures

5 Productive efficiency occurs when:
- A price equals average cost
- **B** ✓ output is produced at minimum average cost
- C price equals marginal cost
- D output is produced at the profit-maximising level
- E price equals marginal revenue

Explanation: If output is produced at minimum AC, the amount of resources used per unit of output produced is at its lowest.

6 A sole supplier of water to households is operating under:
- A perfect competition
- **B** ✓ monopoly
- C oligopoly
- D monopsony
- E monopolistic competition

Explanation: Sole supplier of water is a pure monopoly with 100% of the market. Thames water is the sole supplier of water to many parts of the South East.

7 A single buyer of railway rolling stock is operating under:
- A perfect competition
- B monopoly
- C oligopoly
- **D** ✓ monopsony
- E monopolistic competition

Explanation: A sole buyer of a product is a monopsonist. Monopsonists often have the power to reduce the prices that sellers can charge. They operate in both product & factor markets.

8 A few large companies producing motor cars are operating under:
- A perfect competition
- B monopoly
- **C** ✓ oligopoly
- D monopsony
- E monopolistic competition

Explanation: A market dominated by a few no. of large firms is called oligopoly.

A2 Economics: Multiple Choice

9 A large number of farmers supplying peas at identical prices are operating under:

- ✓ A perfect competition
- B monopoly
- C oligopoly
- D monopsony
- E monopolistic competition

Explanation: A large no. of firms selling a homogenous product such as peas are likely to be an example of perfect competition.

10 A large number of hairdressers in a major city are operating under:

- A perfect competition
- B monopoly
- C oligopoly
- D monopsony
- ✓ E monopolistic competition

Explanation: Hairdressers sell a differentiated product as each has a different stylist & caters for different segments of the market. As they sell differentiated products .: eg of monop comp.

11 In monopolistic competition, which one of the following is true?

- ✓ A the firm has a downward-sloping demand curve
- B the firm has a horizontal demand curve
- C the products sold are homogeneous
- D the firm makes long-run abnormal profits
- E output is always at the productively efficient level

Explanation: Because they can raise prices without losing all of their customers. Also some brand loyalty to certain firms eg hairdressers. All other options do not apply to monop. comp.

12 The table shows cost and revenue characteristics of two firms in long-run equilibrium.

Under which market structures do firms X and Y operate?

	Firm X	Firm Y
	AR exceeds MR	AR exceeds MR
	AC equals AR (Normal profit)	AR exceeds AC (Abnorm prof)
	AC exceeds MC	AC exceeds MC

	Firm X	Firm Y
A	monopoly	perfect competition
✓ B	monopolistic competition	monopoly
C	monopolistic competition	perfect competition
D	perfect competition	monopolistic competition
E	monopoly	perfect competition

Market structures

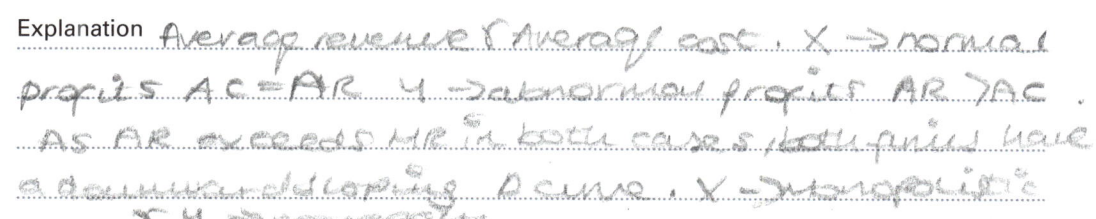

Explanation *Average revenue & Average cost. X → normal profits AC=AR Y → abnormal profits AR > AC. As AR exceeds MR in both cases, both firms have a downward sloping Dcurve. X → monopolistic Y → monopoly*

13 The diagram shows a firm's total cost curve and total revenue curves.

The board of directors is required by the owners of the firm to achieve at least normal profits while also maximising sales revenue. Which level of output will the firm produce at?

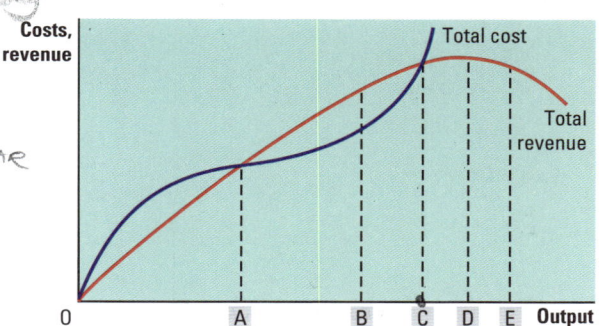

- A
- B
- ✓ C
- D
- E

Explanation *normal profits AR = AC. Point C firm is making normal profits because TC = TR (AC=AR) & sales revenue can rise no further without losses being made.*

14 Under what conditions is the firm described in the table operating?

- A perfect competition and increasing marginal costs
- B monopolistic competition and decreasing marginal costs
- C perfect competition and decreasing marginal costs
- D monopolistic competition and increasing marginal costs
- E monopoly and decreasing marginal costs

Weekly output (units)	Total revenue (£) MR	Total cost (£) MC ↑
1	20	5
2	38 18	12 7
3	54 16	27 15
4	68 14	47 20
5	80 12	77 30

Explanation *MC = rising & MR is ↓. Example of monopolistic comp in SR with Abnormal profits*

A2 Economics: Multiple Choice

15 The diagram represents the cost and revenue curves of a profit-maximising firm operating as a monopoly. Which rectangle represents the abnormal profit of the firm at the short-run equilibrium level of output?

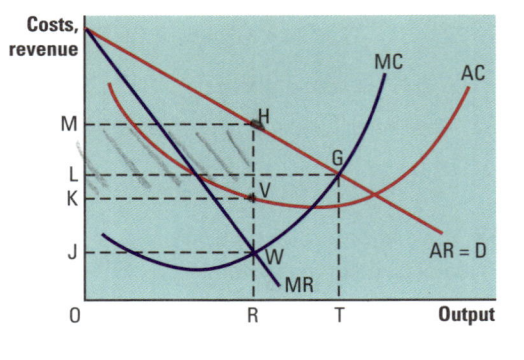

- ✓ A KMHV
- ☐ B OJWR
- ☐ C OKVR
- ☐ D JMHW
- ☐ E OLGT

Explanation: Abnormal profit arises when AR > AC & profit max level of output is at R where MC = MR. AR exceeds AC by VH. If this is × by output OR then Abnormal profit is KMHV.

16 At which output level would this firm maximise its profitable volume of sales?

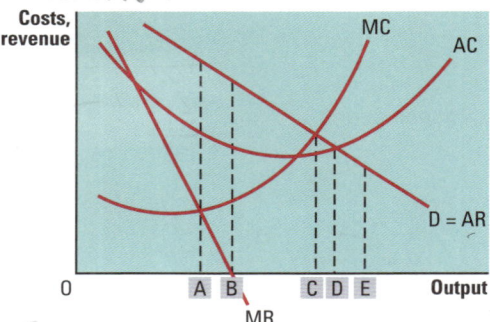

- ☐ A
- ☐ B
- ☐ C
- ✓ D
- ☐ E

Explanation: AR = AC — Normal profits are made. Any output above D would incur losses.

17 A monopoly producer faces a downward-sloping, straight-line demand curve. Which one of the following diagrams correctly depicts its total revenue (TR) curve.

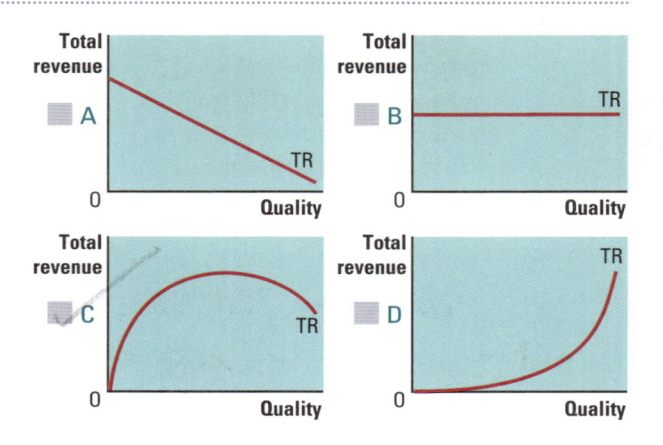

- ☐ A
- ☐ B
- ✓ C
- ☐ D

14

Market structures

will at first rise as demand is elastic & then fall once in inelastic section of D curve. Revenue maximised @ midpoint when elasticity = 1.

18 In order to maximise total revenue, a monopolist should increase output up to a point at which: **MR = 0**

- A marginal revenue equals average revenue
- B price elasticity of demand is maximised
- C marginal revenue is maximised
- ✓ D marginal revenue is zero
- E marginal revenue is minimised

Explanation *downward sloping demand curve is elastic in upper section & inelastic in lower section. Price elasticity = 1 @ midpoint. As a result, as price falls revenue of monopolist will rise. When price & output are set where MR = 0, this means that price & output are at the midpoint of the demand curve. Revenue will thus be maximised.*

19 The diagram shows the marginal and average cost curves and marginal and average revenue curves of a firm in an imperfect market.

Output level X gives:

- A maximum revenue
- B maximum profits
- ✓ C normal profits
- D optimum resource allocation
- E abnormal profits

Explanation *AR = AC. MC curve cuts average cost curve @ its lowest point. X → AR = AC → firm is making normal profits.*

20 A firm in a perfectly competitive market will have a:

- A perfectly elastic supply curve
- B perfectly inelastic supply curve
- C unit elastic supply curve
- ✓ D perfectly elastic demand curve
- E perfectly inelastic demand curve

Explanation *Perfectly elastic horizontal demand curve as it is a price taker. Has to sell its products @ a price determined by market. At any higher price it will lose all its customers as homogenous product with no brand loyalty.*

A2 Economics: Multiple Choice

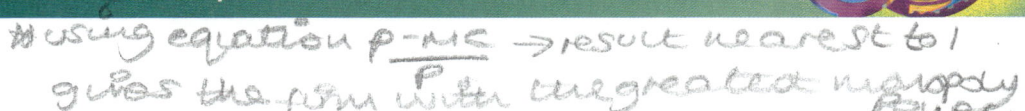

Using equation $\frac{P-MC}{P}$ → result nearest to 1 gives the firm with the greatest monopoly power.

21 The table shows the selling price and marginal cost of five firms, A to E.

	Price	Marginal cost
Firm A	80p	65p
Firm B	95p	35p
Firm C	90p	50p
Firm D	80p	60p
Firm E	70p	20p

Given just this information, which firm has the greatest monopoly power?

■ A ✓ B ■ C ■ D ■ E

Explanation: *Monopoly power can be measured by the extent to which a firm can raise its price above marginal cost ($P = MC$ in p.c market)*

22 An industry having such enormous economies of scale that long-run average costs fall continuously is often called:

- A a monopsony
- B a duopoly
- C a nationalised industry
- ✓ D a natural monopoly
- E an oligopoly

firms ie Network rail & regionalised water companies eg Thames Water are natural monopolies

Explanation: *If an industry has continuous economies of scale, only a monopoly can serve the industry at the lowest possible cost. If there are several small firms competing, cost / unit in each firm will be higher than its a single monopoly.*

23 Which one of the following would tend to increase the degree of monopoly power of a firm?

- ✓ A the extension of a patent
- B a fall in advertising expenditure
- C diversification into other product lines
- D production being concentrated on fewer sites
- E a strengthening of anti-competition legislation

Explanation: *If the no. of years a patent can be used by a firm is increased, it will give it an extension of its monopoly power to sell a product exclusively.*

Questions 24–26 refer to this diagram, which shows five possible output levels, labelled A to E, for a firm.

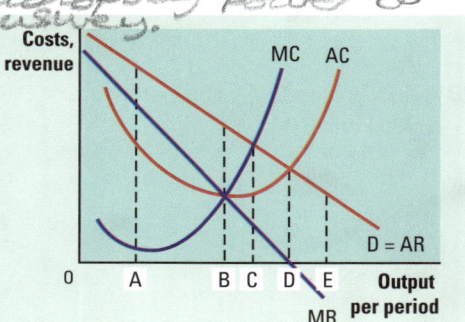

Market structures

24 At which level of output would the firm be making a loss?

☐ A ☐ B ☐ C ☐ D ☑ E

Explanation Loss if AC > AR

25 At which level of output would the firm be maximising its sales revenue?

☐ A ☐ B ☐ C ☑ D ☐ E

Explanation Revenue/sales maximisation
⤷ MR = 0
⤷ output.

26 At which level of output would the firm be maximising its profits?

☐ A ☑ B ☐ C ☐ D ☐ E

Explanation MC = MR → output B → if output rises beyond B, then MC > MR & profits will fall.

27 Under which of the following conditions will a profit-maximising, perfectly competitive firm close down in the short run?

☐ A price is lower than marginal cost
☐ B total cost is greater than total revenue
☑ C average revenue equals average variable cost
☐ D average revenue equals average cost
☐ E price equals marginal cost

Explanation AR or price should be greater than AVC if a firm is to stay in production in the SR. When P < AVC the firm will close down.

28 Monopsony exists in a market if:

☐ A the number of buyers is identical to the number of sellers
☑ B there is only one supplier in a market
☐ C the market has one major supplier
☐ D there is a single buyer in a market
☐ E several sellers market the same product

A2 Economics: Multiple Choice

behaviour. Firms are trying to anticipate their rivals' next moves. Like a game of ~~poker~~ chess with 4/5 players.

How can a monopsonist exploit its market power? *Monopsony can exist in either a product/factor market where there is a sole buyer. Monopsonist is able to force sellers to reduce prices because sellers have only the monopsonist as a customer.*

29 Game theory is mainly associated with which one of the following market structures?

- A monopoly
- ✓ B oligopoly
- C perfect competition
- D monopolistic competition
- E monopsony

Explanation *An oligopoly is a market dominated by few large firms. Game theory allows studying the alternative strategies that oligopolists may choose to adopt depending on their assumptions about their rivals* ✱

30 Abnormal profits can be defined as the:

- A total profits of a firm in a year
- B profit per unit of output of a firm in a year
- C profit required to keep resources in their present use
- ✓ D profit in excess of that required to keep resources in their present use
- E minimum profit a firm requires from producing a given level of output

Explanation *Normal profits AR=AC, when AR>AC, firms make abnormal profits. Firms making A.P. attracts new entrants but barriers to entry may prevent this from happening.*

31 Which one of the following is evidence of a highly contestable industry?

- A continuous economies of scale
- B high set-up costs
- ✓ C firms making normal profits
- D a small number of large firms in the industry
- E capital-intensive methods of production being used by firms

Explanation *No significant barriers to entry or exit. If any SR abnormal profits are made then new entrants will be able to enter the industry easily & compete the profits down to normal level.*

Market structures

32 A motor vehicle manufacturer merging with a retail car distributor is an example of:
- A horizontal integration
- B conglomeration
- C backward vertical integration
- ✓ D forward vertical integration
- E lateral integration

giving manufacturer a sales outlet.

Explanation: A motor vehicle manufacturer acquiring a car distributor is an example of forward V.I. Car dealerships in the UK which only sell one manufacturer's cars are an example of this form of integration.

33 A tobacco firm merging with a computer software company is an example of:
- A horizontal integration
- ✓ B diversification
- C backward vertical integration
- D forward vertical integration
- E lateral integration

Explanation: Conglomerate integration because firm is diversifying in to other activities & spreading risk.

34 A crisp manufacturer merging with a biscuit-making company is an example of:
- A horizontal integration
- B conglomeration
- C backward vertical integration
- D forward vertical integration
- ✓ E lateral integration

Explanation: 2 firms engaging in this form of integration are spreading risk to a degree but also using their joint expertise in areas of common interest. Cadbury Schweppes resulted from integration of food & drink industry.

35 Two budget airlines merging is an example of:
- ✓ A horizontal integration
- B conglomeration
- C backward vertical integration
- D forward vertical integration
- E lateral integration

Explanation: 2 budget airlines eg easyJet & Go a few years ago gives the enlarged firm greater market power & chance to exploit economies of scale.

A2 Economics: Multiple Choice

36 A woollen mill buying a sheep farm is an example of:

- A horizontal integration
- B conglomeration
- ✓ C backward vertical integration
- D forward vertical integration
- E lateral integration

Explanation _Acquiring its supplier of raw materials, which means it is buying backwards in the production process._

37 The following list gives the market shares of five firms in the same industry.

Firm V 25%
Firm W 25%
Firm X 20%
Firm Y 15%
Firm Z 15%

If firms Y and Z merge, the three-firm concentration ratio will become:

- A 50%
- B 60%
- C 70%
- ✓ D 80%
- E 90%

Explanation _Y & Z – combined market share of 30% → 3 firm concentration ratio of 30 + 25 + 25 = 80%._

38 In which of the following activities are there unlikely to be both small and large firms producing the same product?

- A motor vehicle manufacture
- B confectionery
- C brewing beer
- ✓ D oil refining
- E bread making

✗ _mainstream mass market with smaller producers supplying niche markets._

Explanation _✗ capital intensive – with significant economies of scale. Set up costs high, no scope for product differentiation. Other industries have large firms supplying the_

39 If an industry has a five-firm concentration ratio of 90%, this means:

- ✓ A the five largest firms account for 90% of the industry's output
- B 5% of the firms account for 90% of the output
- C 90% of the firms account for 5% of the output
- D five firms account for 10% of the output
- E the structure of the industry is monopolistic competition

Market structures

The firms involved may be tendering for government contracts, result in the government paying out much more than it should. This collusion can give the firms abnormal profits.

Which type of integration increases the concentration ratio?

A horizontal merger reduces the no. of firms & produces a firm with an enlarged market share. E.g. Jet 2 & Go increased market concentration in the budget airline sector in UK.

40 Which one of the following is unlikely to be a motive for horizontal integration in a manufacturing industry?

- A obtaining internal economies of scale
- B rationalising productive capacity
- C obtaining research economies of scale
- ✓ D securing ownership of distribution outlets
- E reducing competition in the industry

Explanation: *example of forward vertical integration*

41 In the state-owned monopoly shown in the diagram, a decision to produce at the socially efficient level of output will require a per unit subsidy of:

- A OX
- B OY
- C OZ
- ✓ D XY
- E YZ

$P = MC$ is socially efficient level of output. → allocative efficient

Explanation: Require a subsidy of XY to keep it in business.

42 If a group of firms in an industry shares out the work available in order to restrict price competition, this is called:

- A exclusive dealing
- ✓ B collusive tendering
- C a cartel
- D patent pooling
- E full-line forcing

Explanation: When a group of firms are invited to submit secret sealed bids for contracts, they may collude to share out the contracts, often at higher prices than if tendering had been done in secret.

A2 Economics: Multiple Choice

The X factor means that regulator allows firms to scope for efficiency improvements & cost savings within the firm.

43 The regulator of a monopoly is using the RPI – X formula and sets X at 5.5%. If inflation in the economy is at 9.5%, the monopoly's prices will:

- A rise by 4% above the country's rate of inflation
- B rise in both nominal and real terms
- C fall in nominal terms and rise in real terms
- ✓ D rise in nominal terms and fall in real terms
- E fall in both nominal and real terms

What is the purpose of setting X?

nominal prices will rise by 4% but in real terms will fall by 5.5% as monopoly prices will rise by less than inflation.

44 If an established firm with significant market power seeks to remove a recent entrant to a market, it might use:

- A limit pricing
- B price discrimination
- ✓ C predatory pricing
- D price leadership
- E marginal cost pricing

Distinguish between predatory pricing and limit pricing.

P - used by established firm to drive a new entrant - with higher unit costs. lower prices so new entrant cannot compete.
Limit - new firms cannot enter market

45 For price discrimination to be effective, all of the following are required except:

- A an ability by the firm to divide a market into sub-markets
- B the inability of consumers to resell the product between sub-markets
- C different price elasticities of demand in each sub-market
- D a degree of monopoly power by the price discriminator
- ✓ E the product must be a necessity for consumers

Explanation *p.d - selling the same product/ service at different prices to different consumers. The product does not need to be differentiated it can be homogenous.*

22

Labour economics

1 In the conditions represented by the diagram, which number of workers employed (A to E) will give the greatest total output?

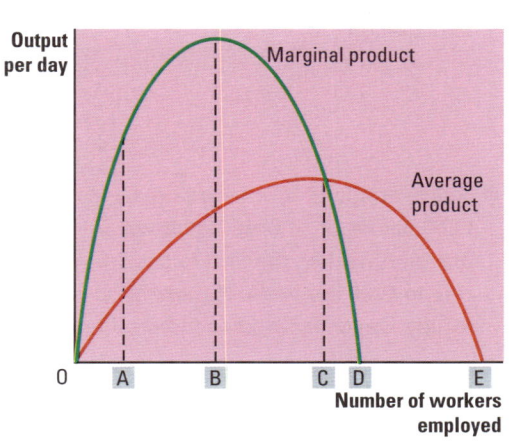

- A
- B
- C
- D
- E

Explanation

2 If a firm is operating in a perfectly competitive market and its product is sold for a price of £2, what is the marginal revenue product of the tenth worker?

- A £30
- B £50
- C £80
- D £100
- E £140

Number of workers	Units of output
8	30
9	60
10	100
11	150
12	220

Explanation

3 The table shows the output for a firm where labour is the only variable factor of production. Diminishing returns will set in with the employment of how many workers?

- A 2
- B 3
- C 4
- D 5
- E 6

Number of workers	Units of output
1	20
2	47
3	76
4	103
5	122
6	132

A2 Economics: Multiple Choice

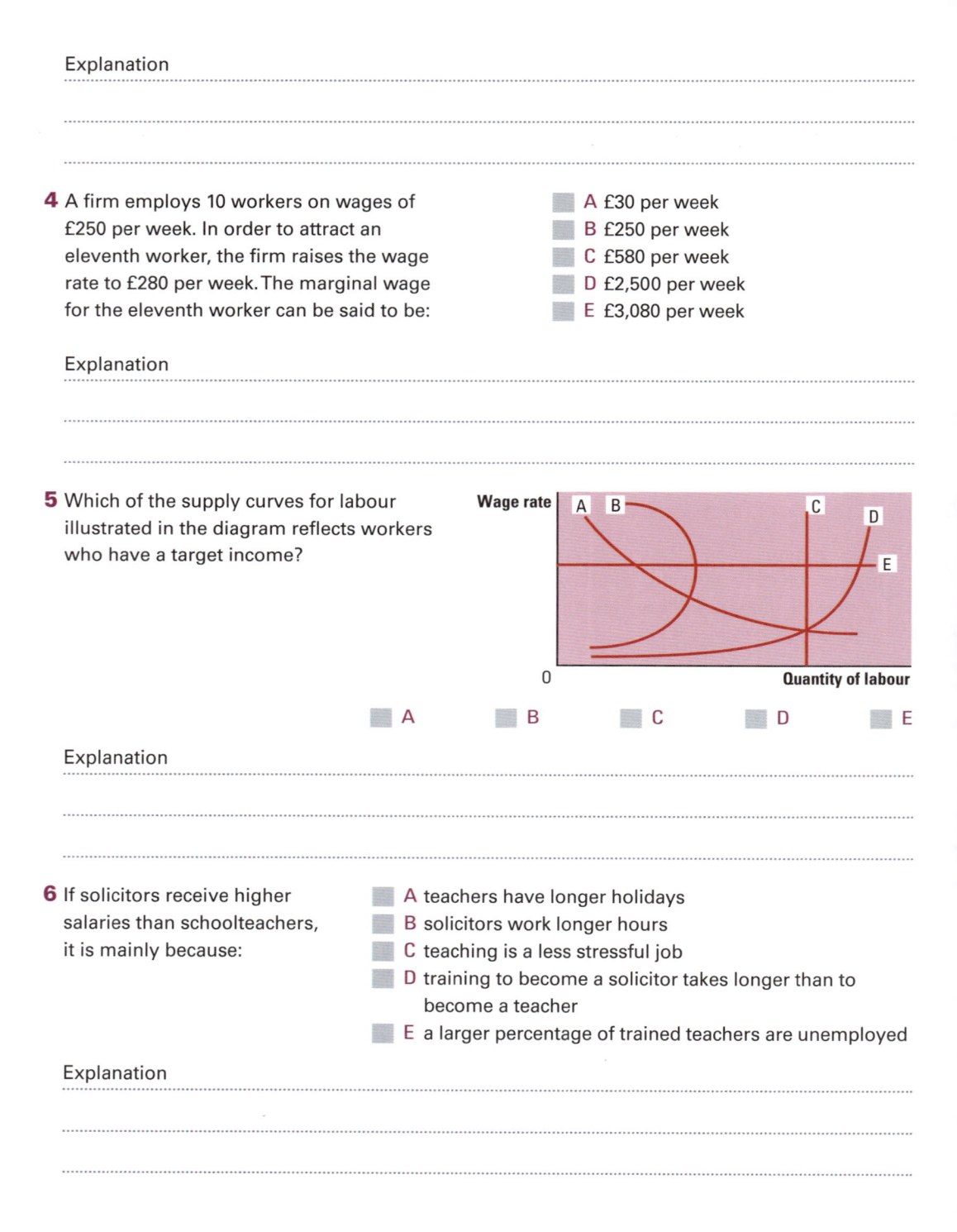

Explanation
....
....

4 A firm employs 10 workers on wages of £250 per week. In order to attract an eleventh worker, the firm raises the wage rate to £280 per week. The marginal wage for the eleventh worker can be said to be:

- A £30 per week
- B £250 per week
- C £580 per week
- D £2,500 per week
- E £3,080 per week

Explanation
....
....

5 Which of the supply curves for labour illustrated in the diagram reflects workers who have a target income?

- A
- B
- C
- D
- E

Explanation
....
....

6 If solicitors receive higher salaries than schoolteachers, it is mainly because:

- A teachers have longer holidays
- B solicitors work longer hours
- C teaching is a less stressful job
- D training to become a solicitor takes longer than to become a teacher
- E a larger percentage of trained teachers are unemployed

Explanation
....
....

Labour economics

7 In which of the following occupations would you expect the supply of labour to have the lowest supply elasticity?

- A railway guard
- B van driver
- C postman
- D architect
- E refuse collector

Explanation

8 The wage rate in an industry is determined by competitive market forces at £4.50 per hour. If the government raises the minimum wage from £4.25 per hour to £4.80 per hour, according to economic theory the result will be:

- A all workers at present in the industry receiving £4.80 per hour
- B no workers being employed at the new minimum wage
- C the supply curve for labour shifting to the right
- D the demand curve for labour shifting to the right
- E some workers receiving £4.80 per hour and some being made redundant

Explanation

9 A trade union is likely to be successful in negotiating a wage increase when:

- A the demand for the product made by the labour is elastic
- B the supply of labour-saving equipment is elastic
- C labour costs are a small proportion of total costs
- D few workers are members of the trade union
- E the price of capital is falling and its productivity increasing

Explanation

A2 Economics: Multiple Choice

10 In the diagram, an industry has the market supply curve of labour represented by XYR.

After a minimum wage of W is introduced, its new supply curve of labour will be represented by:

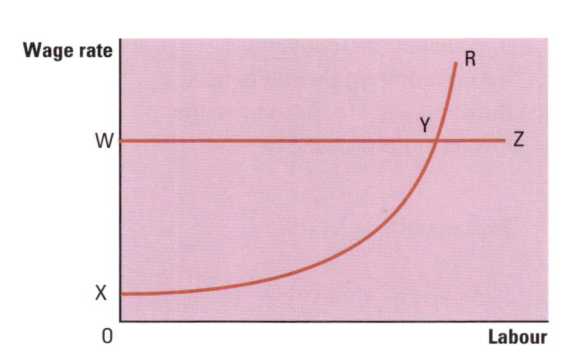

- A XYZ
- B XYR
- C WYR
- D WYZ
- E RYZ

Explanation

11 This diagram refers to the demand and supply of labour in a certain market.

The economic rent earned by the workers is represented by:

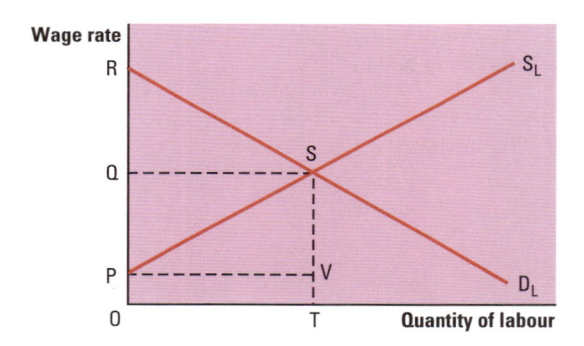

- A RQS
- B QPS
- C SPV
- D POTS
- E QOTS

Explanation

12 Quasi-rent can be defined as:

- A rent on council houses
- B excess profits earned by a monopolist
- C rent earned on property
- D short-term economic rent
- E transfer earnings minus economic rent

What is meant by transfer earnings?

Labour economics

13 The diagram represents a monopsonistic labour market with no trade unions.

The surplus that will be received by the employer is represented by the area:

- A OXSP
- B OYRP
- C XZWS
- D OYTQ
- E PRTQ

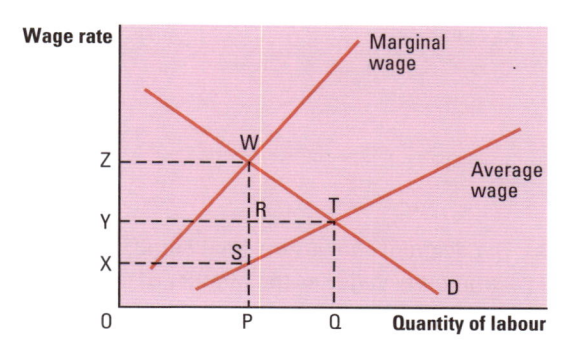

Explanation

14 The shift of the supply curve in the labour market from S_{L1} to S_{L2} could have been caused by:

- A a rise in the wage rate
- B the unionisation of the whole of the labour market
- C the deregulation of the labour market
- D a rise in labour productivity
- E a fall in the price of capital

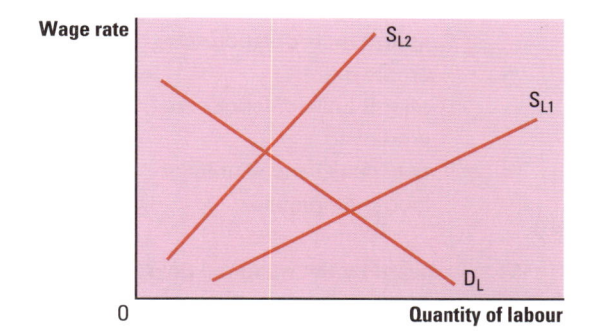

Explanation

15 If S_L represents the supply of labour at its potential level and S_N represents the supply of labour following the inclusion of labour market obstacles, then XY represents:

- A overmanning
- B cyclical unemployment
- C excess demand for labour
- D natural unemployment
- E demand-deficient unemployment

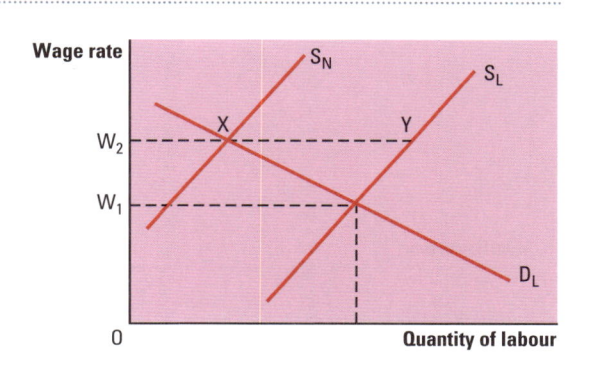

A2 Economics: Multiple Choice

Explanation

....

....

....

16 The diagram shows how total output of a commodity varies as the number of units of labour employed is increased.

Diminishing marginal productivity of labour sets in:

- A from the very first unit of labour employed
- B after Q units of labour are employed
- C after R units of labour are employed
- D after S units of labour are employed
- E between O and Q units of labour employed

What is meant by the marginal physical product of labour?

....

....

....

17 What would be most likely to lead to an increase in the wages of UK bricklayers?

- A an increase in the price of bricks
- B a reduction in interest rates on loans for house purchase
- C a reduction in the apprenticeship period for bricklayers
- D the ending of tax relief on interest for house purchase loans
- E an influx of bricklayers from eastern Europe

Explanation

....

....

....

Labour economics

18 The diagram represents the labour market in a certain occupation.

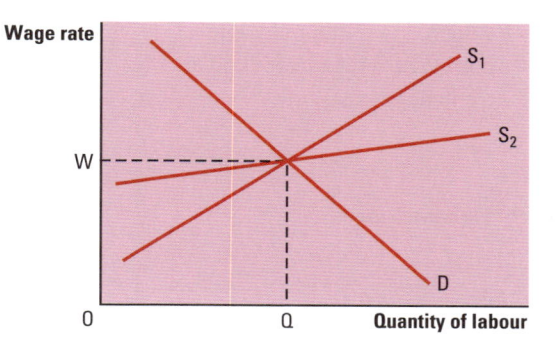

What would be the effect on transfer earnings and economic rent of a change in the supply curve for labour from S_1 to S_2?

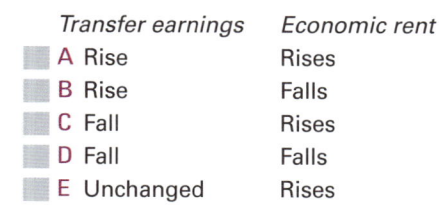

	Transfer earnings	Economic rent
A	Rise	Rises
B	Rise	Falls
C	Fall	Rises
D	Fall	Falls
E	Unchanged	Rises

Explanation

19 In the diagram, if the current wage rate in a firm is W_1 and the numbers employed are Q, the highest wage an entrepreneur would pay is:

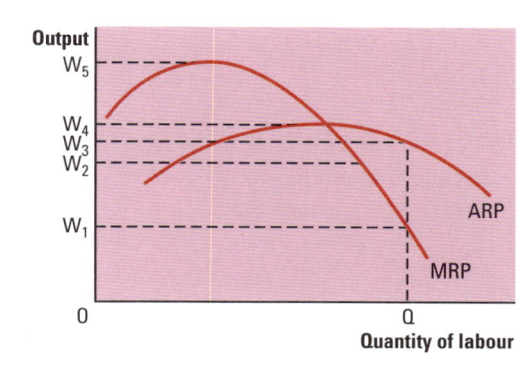

- A W_1
- B W_2
- C W_3
- D W_4
- E W_5

Explanation

20 Occasionally in recent years in the UK, despite positive economic growth, there have been falls in the levels of both unemployment and employment. This could have been due to:

- A more people registering as being available for work
- B fewer young people going into higher education
- C more people working beyond the official retirement age
- D more 16-year-olds taking up full-time employment
- E more people of working age becoming economically inactive

Explanation

Development economics

1 Which one of the following countries is best described as a transitional economy?

- A Sweden
- B Taiwan
- C Romania
- D Sudan
- E North Korea

Explanation

2 Which country is best described as a command economy?

- A Sweden
- B Taiwan
- C Romania
- D Sudan
- E North Korea

Explanation

3 Which country is best described as a less economically developed economy?

- A Sweden
- B Taiwan
- C Romania
- D Sudan
- E Argentina

Explanation

4 Which country is the best example of a mixed economy with a large public and private sector?

- A Sweden
- B Taiwan
- C Romania
- D Sudan
- E North Korea

Explanation

Development economics

5 Which country is best described as a newly industrialised economy?

- A Sweden
- B Taiwan
- C Romania
- D Sudan
- E North Korea

Explanation
....
....
....

6 The economic theory asserting that economic growth depends on increases in its savings rate and decreases in the capital–output ratio is called the:

- A Rostow stages of growth model
- B Prebisch–Singer hypothesis
- C Harrod–Domar growth model
- D Marshall–Lerner condition
- E Marxist theory of surplus value

What is the Prebisch–Singer hypothesis?
....
....
....

7 A widely used measure of the relative social and economic progress of a country is the:

- A human development index
- B human poverty index
- C human suffering index
- D human growth index
- E human employment index

What is the human poverty index?
....
....
....

8 Which one of the following countries is likely to have the highest percentage of people living on less than $1 per day?

- A Brazil
- B Greece
- C Poland
- D Zambia
- E Mexico

Explanation
....
....
....

A2 Economics: Multiple Choice

9 All of the following are characteristics of less economically developed countries except:

- A low factor productivity
- B dependence on the export of primary products
- C low levels of underemployment
- D high population growth
- E increasing urban population

Explanation

10 Which one of the following is the third stage of growth in Rostow's stages of growth model?

- A drive to maturity
- B age of high mass consumption
- C traditional society
- D take-off
- E subsistence economy

Explanation

11 The idea of generating employment opportunities for the abundant labour forces of developing countries is associated with:

- A the Lewis two-sector model
- B the Harrod–Domar model
- C Schumacher's concept of intermediate technology
- D the Prebisch–Singer hypothesis
- E the Marxist theory of surplus value

Explanation

12 The claim that population of a country would grow geometrically while food supplies would only grow arithmetically is associated with:

- A Karl Marx
- B Adam Smith
- C John Keynes
- D Milton Friedman
- E Thomas Malthus

Explanation

Development economics

13 Which one of the following countries is likely to have a human development index (HDI) which is between 0 and 0.3?

- A Turkey
- B Brazil
- C Ethiopia
- D Paraguay
- E Poland

How is the HDI calculated?

....

....

....

14 In order to begin a comparison of living standards between countries, it is best to use the:

- A market exchange rate
- B real exchange rate
- C effective exchange rate
- D purchasing power parity exchange rate
- E trade-weighted exchange rate

Explanation

....

....

15 GNP per capita measured in US dollars may be a poor indicator of comparative standards of living between developed countries and less developed countries because of a divergence in:

- A exchange rates from purchasing power parities
- B population growth rates
- C rates of price and wage inflation
- D ratios of imports to national income
- E inflation rates and unemployment rates

Explanation

....

....

16 The fall in the prices of primary product exports from less developed countries has led to:

- A current account surpluses on their balance of payments
- B a deterioration in their terms of trade
- C a reduction in the level of their international debt
- D a fall in the level of production of primary products
- E rising living standards in developing countries

Explanation

....

....

A2 Economics: Multiple Choice

17 Which organisation provides development funds for less developed countries?

- A Organisation for Economic Cooperation and Development (OECD)
- B World Trade Organisation (WTO)
- C International Bank for Reconstruction and Development (IBRD)
- D Organisation of Petroleum Exporting Countries (OPEC)
- E North American Free Trade Association (NAFTA)

What are the functions of the World Trade Organisation?

....

....

....

18 A developed country imposes a tariff on the product of a less economically developed country (LDC) as shown in the diagram. The price of imports from the LEDC before the tariff is shown as P_i and as P_{i+t} after the tariff.

D_d and S_d represent the domestic demand and supply of the product in the developed country.

As a result of the tariff, the two shaded areas looking left to right represent:

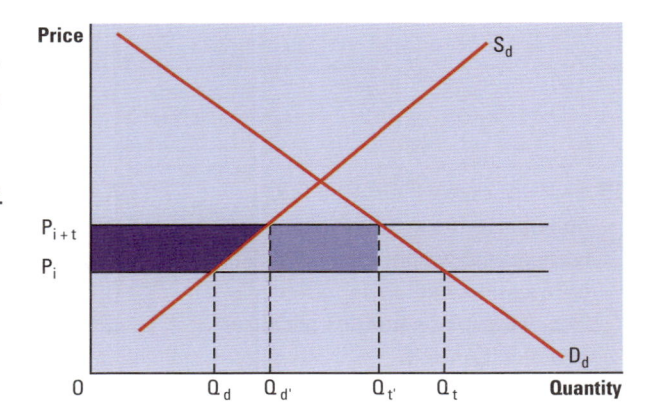

- A gain in consumer surplus and loss of producer surplus
- B tariff revenue and gain in consumer surplus
- C loss in consumer surplus and gain of producer surplus
- D deadweight loss and tariff revenue
- E gain in producer surplus and tariff revenue

Explanation

....

....

....

Development economics

19 Which one of the following areas of the world has the highest percentage share of export earnings from primary products?

- A Australasia
- B Africa
- C North America
- D South-East Asia
- E Eastern Europe

Explanation
....
....
....

20 If a less economically developed country has a GDP greater than its GNP, this could be due to:

- A a depreciation of its exchange rate
- B the repatriation of profits by foreign multinational firms
- C a reduction in the level of aid given by developed countries
- D a fall in the price of the primary products that it exports
- E high levels of emigration by its skilled workers

Explanation
....
....
....
....
....

Macroeconomic policy

1 The table shows a country's level of consumption at various levels of national income.

National income (£m)	Consumption (£m)
20	22
24	24
28	26
32	28
36	30
40	32

What happens to the average and marginal propensities to consume as income increases?

	Average propensity to consume	Marginal propensity to consume
A	constant	constant
B	falls	constant
C	falls	falls
D	increases	falls
E	increases	increases

Explanation
....
....

2 The value of the multiplier would be reduced by:

- A an increase in government investment expenditure
- B an increase in consumption
- C an increase in the standard rate of income tax
- D an increase in the volume of exports
- E a fall in the savings ratio

Explanation
....
....

3 The acceleration principle states that:

- A investment is a function of the level of income
- B income is a function of the rate of change of investment
- C investment is a function of the rate of change of income
- D investment is a function of the rate of interest
- E consumption is a function of income

Explanation
....
....

Macroeconomic policy

4 The value of the accelerator would increase if there was:

- A a reduction in tax rates
- B an increase in the capital–output ratio
- C an increase in the savings ratio
- D an increase in the marginal propensity to consume
- E an increase in interest rates

Explanation

5 In the diagram, X shows the accelerator relationship between net investment and national income.

What determines the slope of the curve?

- A the multiplier coefficient
- B the rate of depreciation of capital
- C the marginal propensity to consume
- D the capital–output ratio
- E the rate of growth of national income

Explanation

6 Which one of the following policies would be used to increase the money supply?

- A a rise in interest rates
- B a rise in the cash ratio requirement for commercial banks
- C a purchase by the central bank of government securities from the banking system
- D a sale by the monetary authorities of government securities to the non-bank sector
- E a rise in the basic rate of income tax

Explanation

A2 Economics: Multiple Choice   37

A2 Economics: Multiple Choice

7 In a banking system, all banks maintain 20% of deposits in cash. One bank receives a new deposit of £200 and there are no withdrawals from the banking system. What will be the final increase in deposits within the system?

- A £20
- B £200
- C £800
- D £1,000
- E £2,000

Explanation

8 If the interest rate is at r/x on this liquidity preference schedule, it can be deduced that:

- A inflation is rising rapidly
- B further falls in interest rates are expected
- C a fall in bond prices is a certainty
- D the velocity of circulation of money is falling
- E incomes must be rising

Explanation

9 The information below relates to an economy:

money supply = £10m
number of transactions = 5m
velocity of circulation = 2

According to the quantity theory of money, the average level of prices will be:

- A £2
- B £4
- C £8
- D £10
- E £50

Explanation

10 What would be the average level of prices in the economy if the money supply were £40m, the number of transactions 10m and the velocity of circulation 4?

- A £4
- B £8
- C £16
- D £20
- E £32

Macroeconomic policy

Explanation

11 Which one of the following is likely to intensify a recession following a fall in aggregate demand?

A unemployment benefit expenditure increasing as the level of economic activity falls
B firms maintaining a fixed ratio of stock to sales
C falling government revenue from excise duties as consumer spending falls
D a falling yield from income tax as incomes fall
E firms reducing their manning levels by natural wastage

Explanation

12 If government spending is growing at a faster rate than the rate of growth of GDP, all of the following could result, except:

A an increase in the money supply
B a rise in long-term interest rates
C an increase in the tax burden
D a decrease in government spending on health and education
E a decrease in resource crowding out

Explanation

13 Which one of the following government policies will cause an increase in the money supply?

A selling short-dated government securities to the banking sector
B a rise interest rates
C selling long-dated government securities to the non-bank sector
D a rise in income tax rates
E an increase in the fiscal surplus

Explanation

A2 Economics: Multiple Choice

14 Which one of the following combinations of problems would be most likely to cause government to increase taxation and raise interest rates if the economy has a fixed exchange rate?

- A demand-pull inflation and low investment
- B demand-pull inflation and a current account deficit
- C low investment and a current account surplus
- D unemployment and a current account deficit
- E unemployment and low inflation

Explanation

15 All of the following would produce an automatic increase in revenue during a period of inflation except:

- A taxes on company profits
- B income tax
- C flat-rate excise duties
- D value added tax
- E capital gains tax

Explanation

16 If the government decided to raise the top rate of income tax from 40% to 50%, this would make the income tax system:

- A regressive
- B less regressive
- C proportional
- D more progressive
- E less progressive

Explanation

17 The term 'poverty trap' has been used to describe a situation when those on low incomes:

- A do not claim all the state benefits to which they are entitled
- B have debts greater than their savings
- C receive such low state benefits that they live below the poverty line
- D have an effective marginal tax rate which is above 100%
- E have an average tax rate which is above their effective marginal tax rate

Macroeconomic policy

Explanation
....
....
....
....

18 During inflation, rising money incomes will automatically pull more people into higher-income tax brackets. This is known as:

    A the poverty trap
    B a negative income tax
    C fiscal drag
    D overfunding
    E reflation

Explanation
....
....
....

19 In macroeconomics, resource crowding out applies to:

    A firms wishing to relocate away from congested areas
    B public expenditure displacing private expenditure
    C low wages leading to workers leaving an industry
    D a customs union causing a loss of exports among non-member countries
    E consumer spending displacing investment spending

What is financial crowding out?
....
....
....

20 All of the following policies would be appropriate in dealing with the natural rate of unemployment except:

    A a reduction in interest rates
    B a reduction in unemployment-related benefits
    C the abolition of the national minimum wage
    D the introduction of travel permits for unemployed workers to search for jobs
    E a reduction in the basic rate of income tax

Explanation
....
....
....

A2 Economics: Multiple Choice

21 In the diagram, the aggregate demand curve has shifted from AD$_1$ to AD$_2$. This is most likely to have been caused by a fall in:

  A interest rates
  B the savings ratio
  C the external value of the pound
  D income tax allowances
  E the basic rate of income tax

Explanation

22 Which one of the following could shift both the aggregate demand and aggregate supply functions to the right?

  A a fall in income tax rates
  B a rise in interest rates
  C a fall in the foreign exchange rate
  D a rise in government spending on benefits
  E a fall in the nominal money supply

Explanation

23 In the diagram, a reduction in which one of the following would have shifted the short-run aggregate supply curve from AS$_1$ to AS$_2$?

  A the natural rate of unemployment
  B the average price of final output
  C the minimum wage rate
  D the value of sterling on the foreign exchanges
  E the rate of interest

Explanation

Macroeconomic policy

24 An assumption made when drawing this short-run aggregate supply curve is that in the economy:

- A money wage rates are fixed
- B real wage rates are fixed
- C real wage rates are flexible
- D both money and real wage rates are flexible
- E the exchange rate of the pound is fixed

What would be the effect of a significant rise in world oil prices on the short-run aggregate supply curve?

....

....

....

....

25 In the diagram, an economy is originally in equilibrium at price level P_1.

SRAS = short-run aggregate supply curve
LRAS = long-run aggregate supply curve
AD = aggregate demand curve

Which one of the following will shift the equilibrium price level to P_2?

- A a fall in government spending followed by a rise in money wage rates
- B a fall in the money supply followed by a rise in money wage rates
- C a rise in government spending followed by a rise in money wage rates
- D a fall in interest rates followed by a fall in money wage rates
- E a rise in government spending followed by a fall in money wage rates

Explanation

....

....

....

....

....

A2 Economics: Multiple Choice   43

A2 Economics: Multiple Choice

26 The diagram shows the relationship between the percentage change in money wage rates and the percentage unemployed in an economy.

Which one of the following is most likely to have caused the short-run Phillips curve PC_1 to shift to PC_2?

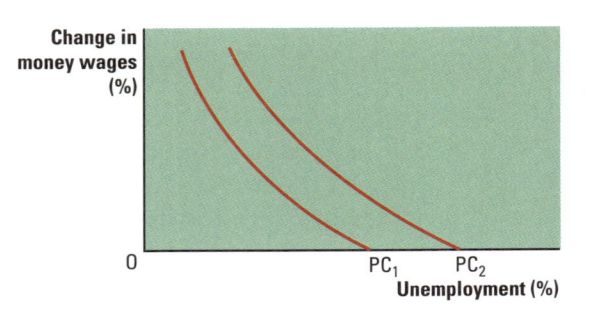

- A a decrease in the natural rate of unemployment
- B a decrease in money wages
- C the expectation of a future increase in the rate of unemployment
- D expectations of inflation adjusting in line with actual inflation
- E a decrease in interest rates

Explanation

27 In the diagram, the long-run Phillips curve has moved from $LRPC_1$ to $LRPC_2$.

This might have been brought about by:

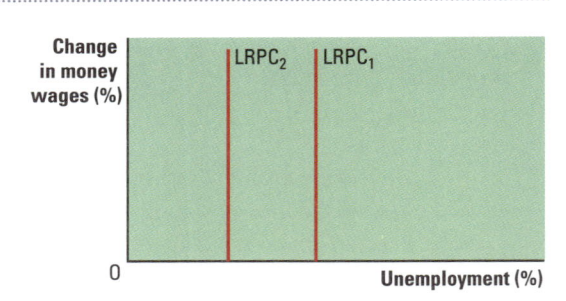

- A a reflationary policy by the government
- B the successful implementation of supply side policies
- C a fall in both the foreign exchange rate and the interest rate
- D a rise in the nominal money supply
- E a rise in income tax rates

Explanation

Macroeconomic policy

28 Natural unemployment can best be defined as:

    A the unemployment caused by a lack of aggregate demand in the economy
    B unemployment caused by a cyclical downturn
    C the unemployment in the economy when the labour market is in equilibrium
    D the total number of people of working age who are economically inactive
    E those who are registered as unemployed but work in the hidden economy

What is the 'hidden economy'?

....

....

....

29 In the diagram, the natural rate of unemployment is A, the economy is at A, N represents the long-run Phillips curve, and PC_1 and PC_2 are short-run Phillips curves.

If the government reflates demand, the route which would be followed according to the expectations-augmented theory would be:

    A AEB   B ADB   C ACD   D ABE   E ABD

Explanation

....

....

....

30 The economic theory associated with a vertical long-run aggregate supply curve, no short-run aggregate supply curves and workers with no money illusion is called:

    A Keynesian demand management
    B the Monetarist expectations-augmented theory
    C neo-classical rational expectations theory
    D Adam Smith's invisible hand of capitalism
    E the Marxist theory of surplus value

Explanation

....

....

....

The global economy

1 The exchange rate of a country's currency measured against a weighted average of the currencies of its major trading partners is called the:

- [ ] A real exchange rate
- [ ] B purchasing power parity exchange rate
- [ ] C nominal exchange rate
- [ ] D effective exchange rate
- [ ] E market exchange rate

Which one of the above best measures international competitiveness?

....

....

....

2 If the monetary authorities in the UK were committed to maintaining the exchange rate of the pound against the euro between P_1 and P_2 in the diagram, what might they do if the demand for pounds rises from D_1 to D_2?

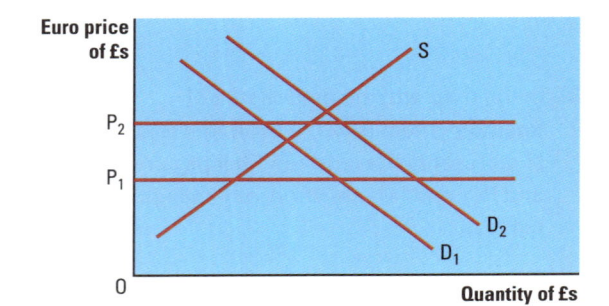

- [ ] A subsidise UK exports
- [ ] B increase interest rates
- [ ] C sell euros out of the foreign exchange reserves
- [ ] D sell pounds on the foreign exchange markets
- [ ] E impose tariffs on euro area goods

Explanation ....

....

....

Questions 3 and 4 relate to this diagram, which shows the demand (D) and supply (S) of pounds. A government is pledged to keep its foreign exchange rate between P_1 and P_2.

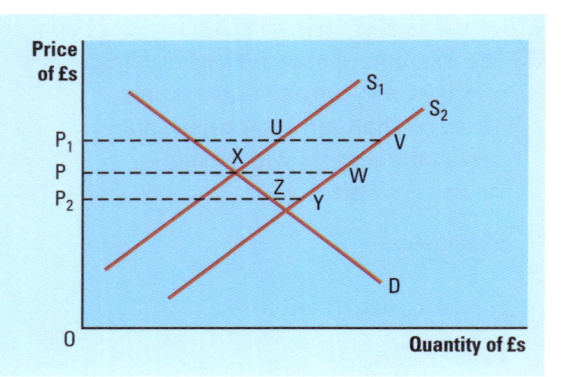

46

The global economy

3 If the supply curve for pounds shifts from S_1 to S_2, this could have been caused by a:

- A rise in exports of goods
- B rise in domestic interest rates
- C fall in exports of goods
- D rise in imports of goods
- E fall in imports of goods

Explanation

4 To keep the exchange rate within the agreed range, the monetary authorities will have to:

- A buy UV pounds
- B sell XW pounds
- C buy ZY pounds
- D sell UV pounds
- E sell ZY pounds

Explanation

5 If the UK monetary authorities wish to achieve an appreciation of the foreign exchange rate of the pound, they could:

- A sell pounds and buy foreign exchange
- B buy pounds and sell foreign exchange
- C sell both pounds and foreign exchange
- D buy both pounds and foreign exchange
- E reduce interest rates

Explanation

6 If the monetary authorities in a country keep the exchange rate significantly above its market level, this is most likely to lead to:

- A high economic growth
- B lower levels of unemployment
- C lower levels of inflation
- D unfavourable terms of trade
- E an improvement in the trade balance

Explanation

A2 Economics: Multiple Choice

7 According to the purchasing power parity theory, the exchange rate between two countries is determined by the:

- A relative price levels in the two countries
- B bargaining power of the respective governments
- C comparative advantage of the two countries in terms of trade
- D relative rates of growth in the money supply in the two countries
- E relative inflation rates in the two countries

Explanation

8 A country imports only one commodity, the price of which is fixed in terms of foreign currency. After a devaluation of its currency by 10%, its imports fall from 50 million to 40 million tonnes. The price elasticity of demand for imports is:

- A –2.0
- B –0.5
- C +0.5
- D +2.0
- E +2.5

Explanation

9 The following price elasticities for exports and imports are for five countries: A, B, C, D and E. If each country's exchange rate depreciates by the same percentage, which country will be most likely to have the biggest improvement in its trade balance?

	Exports	Imports
A	0.8	1.3
B	2.6	1.7
C	1.9	0.8
D	0.3	0.2
E	2.9	1.8

Explanation

10 The value of the US dollar against the pound changes from £0.50 to £0.60. Which one of the following statements is consistent with this information?

- A UK exports to the USA will now be dearer
- B the pound has depreciated against the US dollar
- C UK imports from the USA will now be cheaper
- D Americans visiting the UK will now be worse off
- E UK citizens visiting the USA will be better off

The global economy

Explanation
....
....
....

11 If a country is close to full employment and it experiences a depreciation of its currency, it is most likely to experience a:

    A rise in unemployment
    B fall in GDP
    C rise in the inflation rate
    D fall in aggregate demand
    E fall in tax revenue for the government

Explanation
....
....
....

12 Which one of the following statements is correct for an open economy that has a fixed exchange rate and no exchange controls on capital flows?

    A the growth of the domestic money supply is influenced by the balance of payments
    B the country's inflation rate is unaffected by inflation rates in the rest of the world
    C interest rates are determined solely by the domestic demand for and supply of credit
    D import controls are the only instrument available for correcting a current account deficit
    E the current account will always tend towards long-run equilibrium

Explanation
....
....
....
....

13 The marginal propensity to import is:

    A total imports divided by national income
    B the relationship between a change in national income and the resultant change in imports
    C national income divided by total imports
    D the relationship between a change in import prices and the resultant change in import quantities
    E the relationship between the price of imports and the price of exports

A2 Economics: Multiple Choice

What is meant by the terms of trade?

14 The J-curve effect in international trade is caused by:

- A changes in interest rates
- B cost-push inflation
- C tariffs and other forms of protectionism
- D a significant rise in capital outflows
- E inelastic demand for exports and imports in the short term

Explanation

15 When foreign producers sell at prices below marginal costs, either by making losses or with the assistance of a government subsidy, this is called:

- A trade creation
- B dumping
- C a deadweight loss
- D import substitution
- E trade diversion

What is trade diversion?

16 A government may seek to improve the current account of the balance of payments by introducing either expenditure-reducing or expenditure-switching policies. Which one of the following is an expenditure-reducing policy?

- A a government subsidy on home-produced products
- B a rise in income tax rates
- C a devaluation of the currency
- D the imposition of tariffs
- E the introduction of quotas on imported manufactured goods

Explanation

The global economy

17 A group of countries that work together to remove trade barriers among themselves but have no external tariff is called a:

- A customs union
- B common market
- C free trade area
- D monetary union
- E single market

What is an import quota?

....

....

....

18 The table shows indices of export prices and import prices for a certain country.

Which one of the following statements about the terms of trade during this period is correct?

	Year 1	Year 2	Year 3
Index of export prices	100	105	110
Index of import prices	100	100	120

- A year 3 has the most favourable terms of trade
- B from year 1 to year 2 there was a favourable movement in the terms of trade
- C from year 1 to year 3 there was a favourable movement in the terms of trade
- D from year 2 to year 3 there was a favourable movement in the terms of trade
- E year 1 has the most favourable terms of trade

Explanation

....

....

....

19 Country X joins an existing customs union comprising countries Y and Z. If X's initial tariffs are at the same levels as the customs union's common external tariffs, then joining the customs union is likely to:

- A leave the existing pattern of trade between Y and Z unchanged
- B result only in trade diversion
- C leave the existing pattern of X's trade unchanged
- D result in both trade creation and trade diversion
- E result only in trade creation

Explanation

....

....

....

20 P_w = world price
P_{w+t} = world price plus tariff

Following the imposition of a tariff, what does the shaded area on the diagram represent?

- A tariff revenue for the government
- B revenue for domestic producers
- C revenue for importers
- D the producer surplus for domestic producers
- E the welfare loss as a result of imposing the tariff

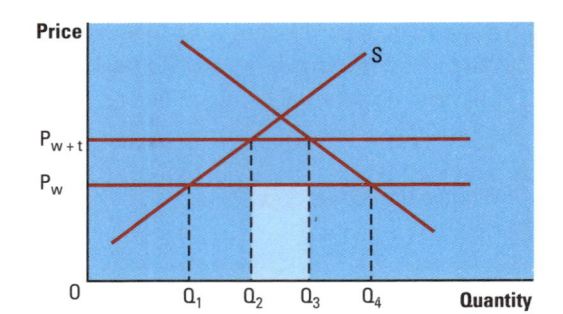

Explanation